Lessons with Geoff Thompson

The Ground Fighting Series

Volume Two

The Escapes

Other books and videos by Geoff Thompson:

Watch My Back - A Bouncer's Story.
Bouncer (the sequel to Watch My Back).
The Pavement Arena - adapting combat martial arts to the street.
Real Self Defence.
Real Grappling.
Real Punching
Real Kicking.
Weight Training - For the Martial Artist.
Animal Day - Pressure testing the Martial Arts.
Tuxedo Warrior - Tales of a Mancunian Bouncer. By Cliff Twemlow. Foreword By Geoff Thompson.
Fear - The Friend of Exceptional People (Techniques in controlling fear)
Dead or Alive - The complete self protection hand book. (As released by Paladin Press in the USA.)

The Ground Fighting series:

Vol One - Pins - The Bedrock.
Vol Three - Chokes and Strangles.
Vol Four - Arm bars and Joint locks.
Vol Five - Fighting from your knees.
Vol Six - Fighting from your back.

Videos - (all videos approx. one hr.):

Lessons with Geoff Thompson
Animal Day - Pressure testing the martial arts.
Animal Day part 2, A deeper look - The fights.
Three Second Fighter - The sniper option.
The Ground Fighting series:
Vol One - Pins, the bedrock.
Vol Two - Escapes.
Vol Three - Chokes and strangles
Vol Four - Bars and joint locks.
Vol Five - Fighting from your knees.
Vol Six - Fighting from your back.

Forthcoming books:

Real Head, Knees and Elbows.
Contemporary Self Protection (released as Dead or Alive in USA)
Blue Blood on the Mat - Athol Oakley - Foreword Geoff Thompson.
On the Door - Further Bouncer Adventures.

Summersdale Publishers
PO Box 49
Chichester
West Sussex
PO19 2FJ
United Kingdom

A CIP catalogue record is available for this book from the British Library.

ISBN 1 873475 71 3

Photographs by Paul Raynor (01484 451115)

ABOUT THE AUTHOR

Geoff Thompson was a doorman for 9 years and has been a practising martial artist for over 20 years. He presently holds a 4th Dan C.E.K.A., 4th Dan B.C.A., 2nd Dan K.U.G.B., 1st Dan Modga Kung Fu, A.B.A. Ass. Boxing Coach, Amateur Wrestling Coach and a B.T.K.B.C. Muay Thai Boxing Coach. Geoff is a former British Weapons Champion and has also trained widely in Aikido, Judo and is qualified to teach Ju-Jitsu. He has frequently appeared on national and international television and radio talking about and giving advice on self protection and related subjects. He is currently the B.B.C. T.V. Good Morning self defence expert. Geoff's first book, Watch My Back - A Bouncer's Story, is fast becoming a cult book. His other books have also been hugely successful. He has been published and commissioned by many publications including G.Q. Magazine, and has written 12 television plays based on his Bouncer books. Geoff is recognised as an international authority on the art of self protection.

Note: With ground fighting techniques the author recommends that you practice only under supervision to avoid accidents and always employ the 'tap system' in practice (if you want to submit or a technique is too painful or you wish to stop practice at any time tap the mat, tap yourself or your opponent with your hand or foot; if this is not possible just say to your opponent 'tap'). If an opponent taps out it is imperative that you release your hold immediately or suffer the consequence of what might be serious injury, and remember, what goes around comes around. If you do not release when he taps he may not release the next time you tap.

Important note
If you have or believe you have a medical condition, the techniques outlined in this book should not be attempted without first consulting your doctor. The authors and the publishers cannot accept any responsibility for any proceedings or prosecutions brought or instituted against any person or body as a result of the use or misuse of techniques described in this book or any loss, injury or damage caused thereby.

ACKNOWLEDGEMENTS
With special thanks to Marc McFann and my good friend and grappling sempai Rick Young.

Contents

Introduction

Welcome to Volume Two in the ground fighting series, The Escapes. Invariably when teaching pins and controlling an opponent on the floor people will ask, 'yea, it's all right knowing how to hold someone down, but what if the opponent gets you in one of these holds, how do you get out of them?' In answer to these people I have written this second volume on how to escape from a bad position.

As with Volume One these moves are useless unless they are drilled to reaction status, they need to be a part of you. Practice at first with a compliant partner to learn technique then cast compliancy away like a pair of redundant crutches and practice against an opponent who is trying, like his life depends upon it, to stop you escaping. If you let your partner escape, or he you, then you are both practising to lose in a real fight. If you end up being pinned on the floor by some maniac rode digger with RSJ shoulders and ten pints of larger inside him you'd better be well practised in your escapes or you will be pinned and bludgeoned, no matter how many dans you have in vertical ranges.

Make your practice as close to the real thing as you dare, then when you make the step from the controlled environment to the street you will not suffer disorientation because that step is only a small one. This book on escapes is not comprehensive, I don't believe that any book really can be, but it is thorough and it is empirical, I could fill a thousand pages with bollocks techniques that look great but would not work against an un-compliant opponent, that's not my way, I'd rather fill less pages but give you something that I know works and that has worked for me.

In the other five volumes in this series there will also be escapes that might not be covered in this text: these will be mostly in the guise of finishing techniques such as strikes, bites, chokes, bars etc. To keep the books categorical I have deliberately left out certain techniques, that could quite easily slip into this text, and put them in a more appropriate volume.

As with the first book, pins, our aim here is not to use strength to escape, though sometimes you may have to, rather to use surprise, distraction, sensitivity and good technique. In practising isolated escapes with a partner it will be very hard to escape when he knows exactly what you are trying to escape with because the element of surprise is lost to you. If, however, you practice the escapes during live ground fighting practice, all of the latter elements will be open to you: you could go for a poke and hook (to be detailed) escape from the scarf hold, if/when the opponent tenses and pushes forward to block the escape he leaves himself open to the climb over escape, in fact he is pulling you into it. So it is important in training not to lose heart if the opponent seems too strong and your escape fails, better to practice escaping from a pin without limiting yourself to one particular escape. What I have also found with many of the techniques that I teach, and people that I have taught, is that if they do not get the technique on the first or second go they abandon it saying that 'it don't work', sometimes it has taken me months and months of repeating and practising to get the feel for a technique, but when I have got it, I've got it for life. It may be that a technique does not suit you or feel right for you and, if that is the case, then there is little point in continuing its practice, but hey, you can't decide that after one session. I've lost count of the amount of people that I have shown a technique and who have failed at the first attempt then said, 'oh I'm just not supple enough for that technique' or 'it doesn't suit my personality/build/style etc.'

When I first started practising triangular leg choke (to be detailed in Volume Three - Chokes & Strangles) I just could not make it work, my legs were too stiff and my calfs kept cramping with the effort of putting or holding the technique on. I felt like abandoning the technique, but rather than lose or abandon what turned out to be one of my strongest finishing techniques I persevered, I got my legs more supple by stretching, I looked into the histrionics of the techniques to find out if I was doing something wrong and, eventually, I was grappling one day and the technique just fell in and my opponent had to tap out very quickly. In fact I have knocked out two or three people with this technique, by mistake, just in demonstration. So persevere. Anyway, I'm going on a bit here so let's get on to the techniques.

Review

For those that have read the first volume of this series I apologise for repeating material that you have already read. I would like, before I start talking about escapes from the various positions, to review quickly the basic pins, because if you do not know them a lot of the speak throughout the text may seem like gobble-de-gook.

I have no intention of actually going into the histrionics of the holds, how to defend them and how to attack from them and the real intricacies, etc. That, as I said, is a volume on its own. I will repeat, though, that the pins are the bedrock of ground fighting and to go on to finishing techniques of a complex nature before learning the imperative basics is a quick way to failing at everything that you attempt.

Master the standing and walking before you try the running and sprinting, the control of the opponent on the floor, via the pinning techniques, is so very, very, VERY important that to miss is, metaphorically, like diving in the water before you have learned to swim.

All I will list in this chapter is the holds themselves with one accompanying illustration so that, if you haven't read the other books and have no knowledge of the 'ground', you'll at least understand the 'speak'.

The Mount Position:
Side Mount, Reverse Mount

The Side Four Quarter

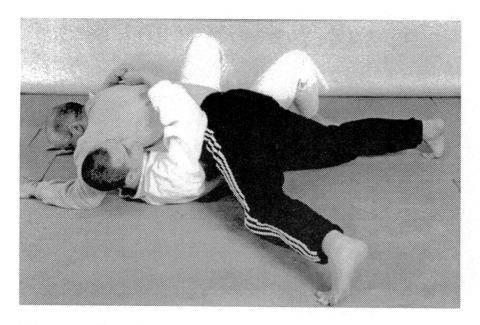

The Scarf Hold

The Jack-Knife

Reverse Scarf Hold

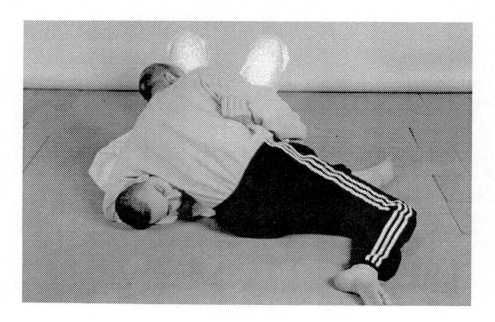

Upper 4/14 Pin

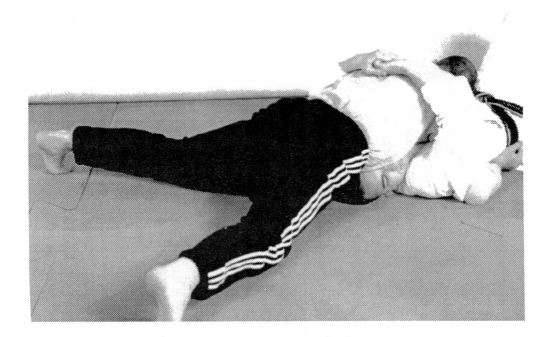

Chapter One

Escapes from the scarf hold

Although someone in the street might not grab and pin you in a text book hold down they will innately grab you in something that closely resembles them. If someone holds you down in a head lock it will very closely resemble a scarf hold and if some one holds you down in a bastardised version of one or two of the conventional pins an abridged version of the appropriate escapes will work just as well.

To start with, and this concerns all of the escapes and is a very important thing to remember, the very best time to escape is the very second that you are pinned, before the opponent has a chance actually to base the pin. That's when he is the most vulnerable, and, because he will probably be falling into the pin, it is very easy to use the momentum of the fall to roll/bridge/turn and escape.

The next best time to escape is when the opponent initiates a finishing move, that is, again, when he's not guarding the pin and so is a good time to escape: when his mind is on a finishing move it will not be on defending his pin. With the experienced ground fighter, who are few and far between and are unlikely to be encountered on the street, that finish may be a technical move like a bar or a turn and strangle (to be detailed in later volumes), with the street fighter that finish is more likely to be a striking finish like a punch/bite/head butt etc.

Between the pin and the finish, if you have not yet found an escape, it is important not to panic because if you do you'll likely tire your self out and lose as a consequence. In fact if you are experienced on the ground (hopefully you will be after reading this six volume series) this is an ideal time to take a rest and let the opponent tire himself out.

Easy to say, I hear you cry, well, let me tell you, with experience you will learn to find resting places on the ground and out wait a hasty, inexperienced opponent. Also, this coolness on the ground will often un-nerve an inexperienced ground fighter, but it only comes with much flight time.

It is also important to realise that this is not a 3 second affair and the ego has to be cast to one side. It may take many minutes, even with an inexperienced, but strong, opponent, to beat him, but when you do it will be a conclusive finish leaving, usually, the opponent unconscious. What tends to happen on the floor is that people rush to finish an opponent because they don't, or their egos don't, want to be seen to be struggling with some guy that has never trained a day in his life.

Often the contemporary martial artist has been indoctrinated into believing that, if a fight takes a while to conclude against an untrained opponent, they have lost face and people will say, 'I thought he was supposed to be good, it took him ages to beat that guy and he hasn't done a day's training, other than in the pub, in his whole life'.

To be honest, if given the choice, I'd rather fight a trained fighter in the street every day of the week than an untrained one, and not because trained fighters are not good, there are some absolute monsters around that's for sure, rather because I know what a trained fighter is thinking and therefore how he is likely to react to certain stimuli because I am a trained fighter myself. He is the devil you know, whereas the untrained fighter is the devil that you don't know, he is so unpredictable, even he doesn't know what he is going to do so how on earth are we going to be able to predict it?

So don't be in too much of a hurry, it may take time, but, as long as you win that is all that matters; there is no room for egos in the world of real. If you are unsure of the technicalities of the pins that we are covering please refer to Volume One in the series, The Pins.

Note:
Reverse the instructions in the following techniques to practice from the opposite side.

Escapes from scarf hold
1) Immediate turn out and Mount. As already stated the best time to escape is the instant that the hold is going on, as the opponent falls into the scarf hold and tries to place his right arm around you head push it, at the elbow, in front of your face slip from underneath him and mount him from the back (as per illustration).

2) Immediate bridge and roll

Using the downward momentum of the opponent as he falls into the scarf hold simply place your arms around his torso and roll him over your chest before he has a chance to base the pin. From here go into a side mount from where you can punch him in the head or face, or poke him in the eye/neck to release the arm from around your head. The opponent is now perfectly positioned for several arm bar techniques, a turn and choke, or a punch out.

3) Box protection and rest

If the opponent has secured the hold use the box protection and take a quick rest for assessment. Turn immediately onto your right side, bring your left arm over and in front of his face so that the bone of your wrist is barring into his face, make a bridge by holding your left fist with your right hand and securing the right elbow on the floor. This will stop the opponent being able to apply any real pressure to his hold and give you vital seconds to secure an escape.

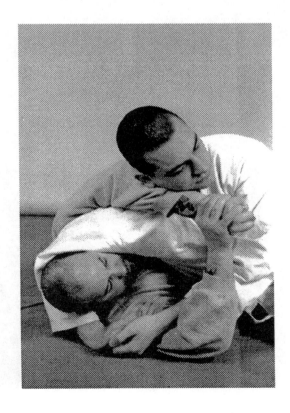

4) Throw legs and sit up

This is not the strongest escape in the world but it has worked for me, if nothing else it is very good to use in conjunction with other techniques as a faint, etc. Simply throw your legs up and slightly behind you, use the momentum as the legs come back down again to sit up, sit through and escape into a scarf hold of your own.

5) Leg tie and bridge

Turn onto your right side and hug your left arm around the opponent's waist, join it up, if possible, with your right arm. Hook the opponent's left (reverse) leg with your right leg and pull in underneath you. From here bridge as high as you can, into a crab, and roll the opponent over your own chest. From here you have the choice of going in to the mount position or a scarf hold.

6) Jack-knife turn

Turn straight onto your side and form the box protection, only this time really push the opponent's face/neck/throat with the bone of your left wrist, this will force the opponent's head to push upwards and back. Simultaneously move your chest away from the opponent's back in to a jack-knife position then push harder with the left arm. As the opponent falls back sit through into the mount. It is important with this technique that your timing is right: if you move into the jack-knife position too soon the opponent will feel your movement and move with you. Use the distraction of pushing up with your left arm to hide the fact that you are separating your chest from his back.

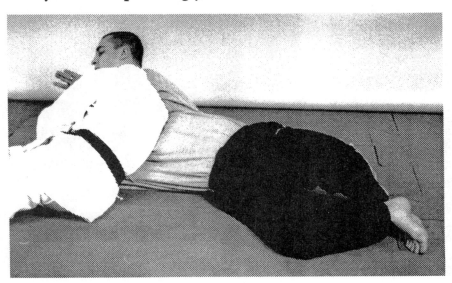

7) Pinch and grab

Place your left arm around the opponent's waist and position it just by his lower ribs, move your right arm to the same position, from the front, and pinch the skin by his ribs or even poke or punch the ribs. When the opponent moves his left hand back to remove/stop the attacking hand grab his wrist with your right hand and then quickly exchange hands by wrapping your left hand around his wrist and locking the arm in position. Push his left elbow with your right hand and bridge and roll the opponent over your chest. From here take the mount position or the side 4 1/4 or the scarf hold. Make sure that when you attack the opponent's ribs you cause enough pain/discomfort to make him want to stop you or the technique will not be employable.

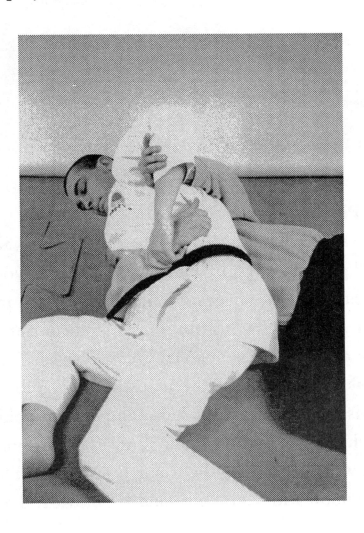

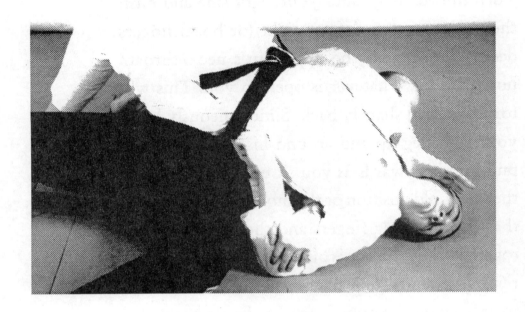

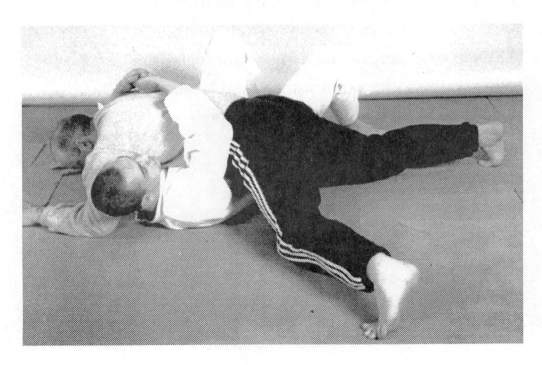

8) Poke and Hook

Turn immediately onto your right side and push the points of your left or right (or both) fingers deeply into/under the opponent's neck/throat/nostrils/eyes, whatever is open to you. This will force his head sharply back. Simultaneously hook your right leg up and around his neck/head and pull him backwards as you sit up, from here take the scarf hold position or the mount. It is important that the attacking fingers and the right leg work together, if the timing is out a strong opponent will remove your fingers and further secure his hold, so as soon as the opponent's head goes back your right leg should already be there ready to hook it. The element of surprise is an important ingredient in this escape so if you mistime it and it fails it is unlikely to work on the second attempt.

Squeeze Out

This is a crude and laboured escape but, if it is all that is left you, you'll be glad to take it. After a lot of wriggling around and unsuccessful attempts to escape your opponent's grip often weakens and it is possible actually to squeeze your head out of his grip and escape from underneath leaving you ideally positioned to employ a reverse mount.

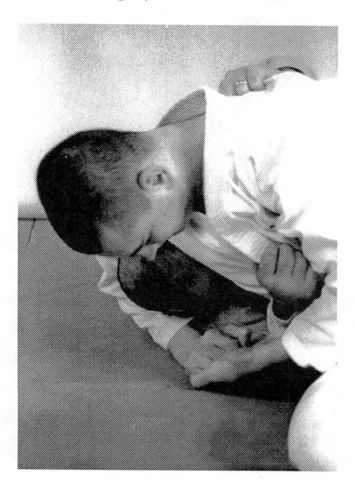

9) Bite and bridge

If you thought the last escape was crude then this one is even worse. I initiate a lot of my escapes by using the bite to cause enough distraction for me to escape. In this case position yourself on your right hand side and place your arms around the opponent's waist, ready for a bridge. Bite him on any available or open part of his torso or head and be sure to try and get just the surface skin so that the pain is more intense. The second that the opponent reacts to the pain use the distraction to bridge hard and roll him over your chest. From here take the mount of the side 4 1/4 or the scarf hold.

10) Climb over

Turn onto your right hand side and wrap your right leg over the opponent's reverse left leg, grapevine it and then climb over him and onto his side or back, depending upon how far he rolls. He will probably still be securing your head, so punch him in the head or face very hard until he releases or poke your fingers into his nostrils/neck/throat/under the jaw-line/eyes and push up with your back until the grip is released. From here finish with an arm bar, punch out, turn and choke etc.

If, as I said earlier, any one of these particular escapes is not working for some reason then it is easy, with practice to combine them to secure an escape. For instance if I go for a climb over escape and he moves his left leg away from me to evade the escape he will be leaving himself open for a hug and bridge because he has redistributed his weight, to evade the climb over, in such a way that he is vulnerable to being bridged. If I try to bridge the opponent will move his weight forward to block the bridge and literally pull me into a climb over. Combining is easy as long as you remember to use an escape that will fit with his blocking re-distribution otherwise you'll do nothing but tire your self out and tiredness makes cowards of us all. At the risk of repeating myself (no, not you Geoff!) these escapes need to be drilled to instinct status if they are to work against an un-compliant enemy.

Chapter Two

The Mount Position

The mount is probably the most common, and innate, position that you are likely to find yourself in, in a real encounter. If you meet an opponent who knows how to defend the position you're in for a real hard and bloody time, though this is unlikely because basing is an acquired technique that few but the dedicated acquire. Having said that, against a determined opponent who is intent on punching you out, it is very easily done from this position.

You will not get out of the mount on instinct alone, you'll need a repertoire of different escapes, ones that are time honoured and practised under pressure, in your curriculum.

Once you do understand, and have flight time in the escapes, this position is not near as scary. I remember talking to a good friend of mine one day, a smashing chap called John Skillen, who is a member of the national Judo team, and he was telling me that he hated fighting from his back. A few minutes later I stood watching him grapple with the lads on the course and, every single time, he automatically went onto his back and fought the fight from there. By confronting his dislike for back fighting he later gained desensitisation to it and it became a strong point.

It is generally only the things that we are unfamiliar with that scare us. Once you have got flight time fighting on the floor not only will it be less daunting it will also become very exciting as you learn, find and perfect new techniques.

1) Immediate Bridge

As with the last pin the best escape is an immediate escape using the opponent's momentum, or the momentum of the fall, and attacking the pin before the opponent has the chance to properly establish it. Even an untrained fighter will automatically base with his hands when you bridge so, when possible, grab his arm or arms so that he cannot base. If you bridge to the left grab his left arm, if you bridge to the right grab his right arm, if you bridge behind then try and grab both his arms.

2) Rest Out

If immediate escape is not an option or the option has been lost then secure the opponent in a head lock, as per illustration, and rest out until the time is right to escape. Try not to over-tense, just use enough muscle strength to hold the opponent: it is very easy in these positions to over exert oneself and end up knackered.

Keep the opponent as close to you as possible, especially his head. This will disable any attempts he may make to use atemi strikes. If the opportunity arises use atemi yourself to weaken the opponent and possibly force him to adjust his weight/position - this will leave you a nice opening to bridge and escape.

I have actually finished fights, using biting technique, from this position because very few people are trained to defend against biting techniques. If, from this rest position, the opponent tries to pull up to break your grip and attack don't resist: as he pulls up, let him pull you up with him so that it is him getting tired and not you. If you try to fight him when he pulls up you will do little more than completely exhaust yourself, once your energy has gone your fight will probably follow. You won't be able to hold this position forever, it is only a traveller's rest position that allows you to have a breather and think of an escape plan. Eventually he will break the grip and you'll be very vulnerable to his atemi strikes. To keep the grip tight interlock both your hands, as illus, and be careful of biting techniques used against you.

2) Arm-leg tie and bridge

A simple and yet very effective method of escape from the mount position is to tie off the opponent's right arm and right leg and bridge into a high crab position, to the right hand side, and roll the opponent off, as per illustration.

It is very important that you tie off both the arm and the leg before bridging: if you tie off only one or the other the opponent still has a means of basing. If you tie off his leg he can base out (defend the pin) with his arm and vice versa. It is easy to tie off the leg, you just move your own foot back to cover his, he probably won't even know that you've done it. Tying off the arm however can be a bit of a struggle so I recommend that you tie off the leg first, preferably without him knowing, and then, as soon as you lock off his arm, bridge immediately. Timing is important if you want the bridge to be effective.

The best way to tie off his arm is to grapevine yours around his. Make sure that you bridge in the same direction as you tie off, if you tie off his right side and then bridge to his left it will have no effect, other than to waste your energy, because he will base with his opposite side.

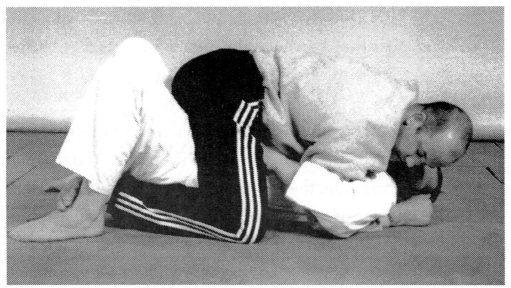

3) Crawl through

This can be an effective, though often elongated escape. It is especially effective if you are struggling to bridge the opponent. Use the points of your fingers to poke into the groin area of the opponent. There are many nerve points on the body that are very sensitive to poking and striking and will move an un-compliant opponent, and the groin area is one of them.

Start on one side, any one, and push at the groin until the opponent's leg straightens. When it does wrap your leg around it to hold it in place then go to work on his opposite side. When that leg straightens tie it off with your other leg. You now have the opponent in your guard (the Ju-Jitsu scissor guard). If you pull your legs back, and shuffle back also, and place them on the opponent's thighs or into his groin you will be in the Judo guard from where escape is much easier and arm bars and leg chokes are available to finish (as detailed in vol 5 fighting from your back).

4) Broken arm tie-elbow/chin push

A good means of resting is to tie off the opponent's left or right arm to disable it from atemi striking by pushing it across your body and trapping it. This is very viable when the opponent over stretches with an attack or a throat grab etc.

As his right arm comes towards your face, or when it actually grabs your neck/throat, knock it across by hitting his right elbow with your left hand. As he falls forward secure the position by wrapping your left arm around his neck, joining it to your right arm, as illus, and forming a temporary head lock. Once in this position you can rest if you need to though escape at this point is a better option because it is not strong enough to hold for any length of time.

To escape using the opponent's elbow first grab his trapped right hand with your left hand and pull it tight, forming a semi-choke using his own arm, then bring your right hand down under his right elbow and pushing hard, up and over. This will force the opponent onto his back. Or, this is my particular speciality, reach over with your left hand and grab the opponent's nose or the inside of his lip, being careful not to go too close to his teeth, and wrench his face to the left. This will definitely move him, and as he follows the pain whip your right hand under his chin and push in the same direction. The opponent will roll onto his back.

Once you have trapped the opponent's arm in the first instant he is very vulnerable to small head butts and finishing bites to the ears or face or neck.

5) Bridge behind and grab arm/s

Bridge high and directly backwards going onto the balls of your feet for maximum effect. This will throw the opponent directly and violently backwards forcing him to base using both hands (if he does not he will be thrown off any way). Anticipating his instinctive base reach back and grab one or both his hands to disable his defence then bridge again. His base is now blocked and he will easily be thrown over. If the opponent only bases with one arm then grab that one and, on the second bridge go to the direction, left or right, of the said arm so that he has no means of defence.

Bite and bridge

This is another particular favourite of mine because no matter where you are there seems to be something that you can bite. What the bite does, or any attack using a pain point, is cause an automatic reaction in the opponent and what this reaction does is take his mind temporarily off his defence: in that split second of reaction we bridge the opponent off.

As stated earlier I find the bite more effective if you bite the opponent in the outer layers of his body where it will pain him most - this will give you a better reaction. Bite the opponent's chest/nipple/arm/stomach etc (whatever is on offer), and as soon as he reacts bridge high and roll him off.

As with most escapes these can be used in combination with one another, if one does not work it will, at least, force the opponent to react by adjusting his body weight, thus leaving him vulnerable to another escape. This will only work for the practitioner who has the escape deeply embedded into his repertoire so that he can feel the opponent's energy and go with it as opposed to against it. If I bridge to the left and feel his energy block me to the right then I will instinctively bridge over to the right and let his energy assist me in my escape.

At an advanced level you can feint or draw the opponent by pretending to try and escape one way in order to get him to move the other way to block, as soon as he does so you go with the flow and the escape is yours. Sometimes, when ground sensitivity is highly developed, you will feel the opponent's intentions and easily escape when he adjusts from one pin to another or moves in for a finish.

The best escape is the one that comes without any effort. In a way we only take what the opponent gives us, so instead of chasing and fighting for a move we wait for him to present us with one. I know that this might be above the head of some people but, when flight time is yours you will understand better.

Ground fighting is a game of chess. We can feint or draw an opponent by offering an incentive or we can manipulate his mistakes by reading his intentions. If I am fighting with an experienced fighter I may offer him the opportunity of taking an arm bar, and when he goes to take it I will go with the move and escape. But, that is all later, for now get the basics down and make them yours before moving on to greener pastures.

Chapter Three

Escapes from the
side 4 1/4 Hold down

The side 4 1/4 is one of the pins that I class as a traveller's rest hold, that is they do not have brilliant finishing potential, although an advanced player will and can finish from here.

Usually the side 4 1/4 is used to get to the more potent pins like the scarf hold or the mount or even to get back to a vertical position once again. That's not to detract from the pin itsself which is a brilliant controlling position that can be held for a good duration without too much effort. In volumes 3 and 4 of this series I will show you some good finishing moves from here, and all the other base pins.

The first time you look at this hold it seems as though there are no real possibilities to escape and one simply has to wait for the opponent to move to a position where there are escapes, when you dig a little deeper however there are some very good escapes.

1) Immediate bridge

If possible the best time to escape is immediately, as soon as the opponent lands in, or finds the hold bridge violently onto the balls of your feet and throw the opponent off, either behind you, in which case you bridge backwards or to the side (the opposite side to where his feet are) in which case you bridge high and over to that side. If this option is not there or it has been spent rest out, don't waste energy trying to move the immovable.

If you are fighting an experienced guy (to be honest the only time, realistically, that you are going to be fighting an experienced ground fighter is in training) he will most likely take a rest here before moving to a more potent position.

If you are fighting a guy on the street he will most likely move very quickly into a position where he can punch your face in, this will usually be the mount. Again, if and when he does move, bridge straight away before he can defend the position. If he is having a rest you can have a rest also, just stay sensitive to his movement so that you can pre-empt any menacing intentions that he may have. Resting doesn't mean having a kip, it means relaxing the muscles but keeping the brain alert.

2) Leg tie and bridge

Turn onto your side, into the opponent, and poke your right fingers into his groin area, or anywhere sensitive. This will force him to move slightly away from your fingers and towards your legs.

Hook his right leg under you with your right leg and then grapevine it with your left leg and tie it off, bridge and roll to your own left to escape.

3) Hug and bridge

Feed your right arm under the body of the opponent and feed your left arm over the top, join both your hands together, bridge and roll the opponent behind or to the left of you (depending upon his energy, whichever way he tenses or pushes that is the way you should bridge).

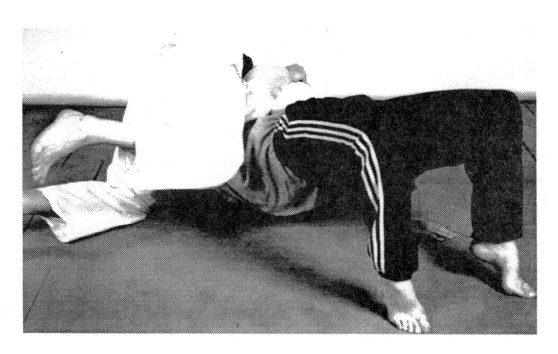

4) Sit up & bridge

If the opponent is holding you in the side 4 1/4 with his left arm around your neck, try to sit up. He will adjust his weight to try and push you back down again as he does so use the energy that he is feeding you and the momentum to sit back and immediately roll over to your left. The harder you try and sit the harder he will try and push you back down again and thus the more energy he will put into your escape bridge.

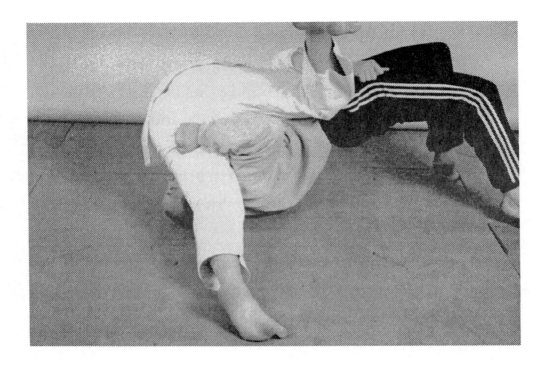

5) Pinch and bridge

Pinch, poke or strike the opponent on his back/
side or in his neck/eyes. When he reaches over to
stop you grab his hand with one hand and push his
elbow with the other, at the same time bridge and
roll him off. It doesn't really matter where you
attack the opponent as long as you inflict enough
pain to divert one of his hands to stop you, when
he does grab the said hand and use it to secure your
escape.

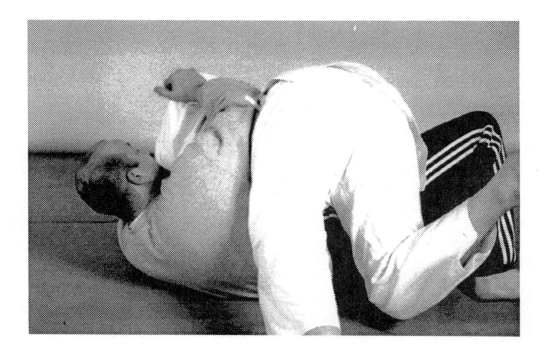

6) Groin grab & bridge

The opponent's groin is very easy to grab from this position and whilst I don't expect to use it as a finishing technique it will definitely move the opponent, this will give you the energy you need to bridge. Reach under the opponent's body and get a grip on his testicles. As he moves (believe me he will move) immediately bridge.

There are also some good leg choke finishes from this position that we will detail in Vol 3. Use these escapes singularly or in combination to secure escape but use the drills detailed later in this text to ingrain the technique so that the thought process does not hamper your escape. If your have to think too long about how to do a certain escape the opponent will read your intentions and easily block you. If, however, you know the techniques inside out you can feint with one escape to force the opponent to block and then initiate another, using his energy.

One of the biggest things with ground fighting is how exhausting it can be so it is imperative to learn to take rests when an immediate escape is not possible, conserve your energy for when an escape is possible. If you are uncontrolled on the floor and buck and bronk and go wild when the chance of escape is not there, you will, within a very short space of time become nothing more than a punch bag. Learning to find resting points and actually taking rests when they are open to you takes a lot of flight time so try and get as much scrimmage (live grappling) in as possible. Calmness under pressure is the reward that you get for putting in hundreds of hours practise.

Chapter Four

Escapes from the upper 4 1/4 Hold down

As with the side 4 1/4 hold down, the upper 4 1/4 is more of a traveller's rest pin than a finishing hold, though, again, the experienced player will find many finishes from here: arm bars, chokes etc (detailed in Vols 3 & 4).

It is an excellent resting place, a good position to get back to your feet and also ideal if you want to move to the more potent mount position. A strong opponent will hold you in this position all day long if you do not have any escape strategies and whilst there are not so many from this position, the few we have are very effective.

As with the side 4 1/4 pin I am never in a great hurry to escape from this hold because it is so easily defended, if I can't escape straight away, which is always number one option, I am happy to place the onus on the opponent to make his move and offer me the means of positive escape rather than burn myself out bucking and bronking. Whilst I am in an unfavourable position I know that, unless the opponent is a very experienced ground fighter, he is going to struggle to do anything other than pin me in this position.

When he makes his move to a different position, usually a position where he can strike from, I'll make my move to escape. If however we have met a stalemate and the guy is happy to hold me there and do nothing else then I will take the onus and start forcing him to move with biting or striking techniques.

1) Immediate bridge
The very second that the hold goes on is the time to bridge high and roll to your left or right and escape the pin. If this is not an option or the option

has been spent rest out being sure to keep your head to the side so that the opponent cannot block your airways and smother you out.

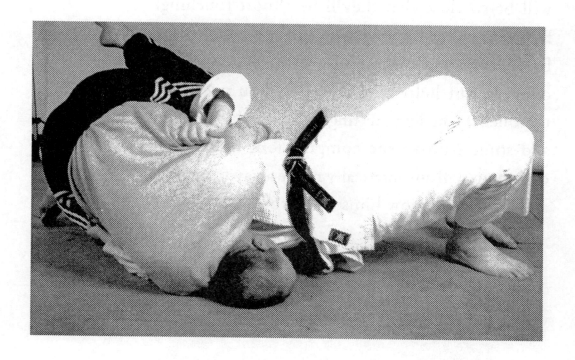

2) Bench press & bridge

Bring your arms in as close as possible and place your palms on the opponent's chest. Your hands will be so close that they'll be almost touching. Bench press the opponent up and at the same time bridge high and turn, left or right, the opponent over. It can help here if, when you press the opponent, you dig your finger tips into his ribs and add some pain to the computation. Usually an opponent will automatically move away from pain and, in effect, throw himself off you.

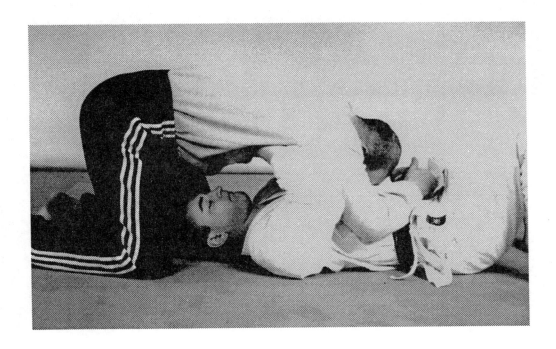

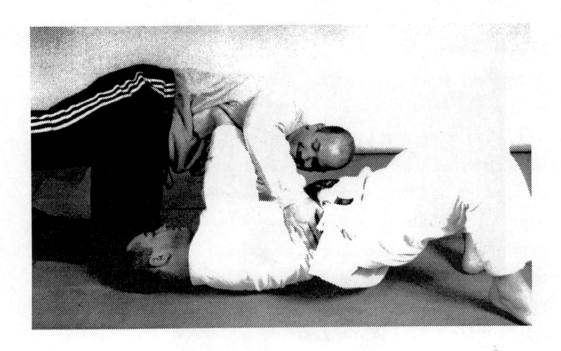

3) Larynx grab and bridge

Feed your hands around to the opponent's throat and poke your fingers, from both sides simultaneously, into his larynx. Whilst you may not have the leverage to choke him out from this position it will cause a pain reaction that you can use to bridge and escape. As soon as the opponent reacts to the pain immediately bridge him off.

4) Grab groin and bridge

Reach under the opponent and grab his testicles:
he will react, and when he does immediately bridge
high and roll to the left or the right, according to

his energy. This also applies with any other pain inflictions that you put on the opponent. As a rule of thumb people will move away from pain so if you want to move or bridge an opponent to the left push the pain in that direction and, when he moves away to avoid the discomfort take the initiative and bridge.

If the opponent reacts by grabbing the hand that your are attacking him with, grab his hand and use it by twisting the joint of the wrist of elbow or shoulder, in the direction of escape and, again, escape in that direction. If at any time you feel it is possible to attack the opponent with bites, butts, gouges, claws, atemi strikes etc do it. Even if it is just to weaken or move him it will be worth the effort. The eyes are especially vulnerable so should be attacked at every and any opportunity. Bites are also excellent moving and finishing techniques.

Don't be squeamish: if your safety depends on it, or your life depends on it or the safety/life of one of your loved ones, just do it. You don't have to bite to sever or gouge to blind to secure an escape -

often a minimal attack to these vulnerable areas is enough to move an opponent enough to secure escape. People are also very reluctant to grab an opponent's genitals: don't be, these people will bring no such morality or squeamishness into battle with them so neither should you. If you restrict yourself socially, sexually or morally then the chances are these limitations will be your undoing. If the genitals are open to attack then bite, butt, knee, punch, claw, rip and crush them without demur.

If you think that this is a little over the top WAKE UP, this is the real world. Martial art means designed for war. War is that nasty place where people blow other people to pieces without batting an eyelid. Confrontations in the street are not fisticuffs, they are also wars where people die as a consequence of not being ready. We all know that violence is wrong and that it is not the long term solution (though it is the short term solution) but the long term solution is not a personal problem it is a social problem - so if it works, use it, you can't put out a big fire with a little bucket.

Chapter Five

Drilling the Escapes

This is where you feed the techniques into the brain computer so that, when spontaneity takes the reigns in a real fight, they will be feed back out in a usable format. You can only get off this disc what you put on it so drill to distraction, you need to know multiple escapes and finishes from every angle of the body so that you are never left thinking 'how the hell am I going to get out of this position?'

Drilling is isolating an escape (or any technique) and repeating it again and again until you are absolutely one hundred per cent pig sick of it - then you'll be good at it. Check out any of the brilliant people of any century and you'll find that they all worked the same way, they repeated a technique thousands, tens of thousands even millions of times to make it a natural reaction, they look at it from every angle and from every conceivable position, they place it under varying forms of pressure to see how it stands up to adversity.

I remember reading about the great golfer Jack Nicholas practising a ten foot put`t on the green, one of his friends noticed him there early in the morning when he was on his way out to play a round of golf. When he came back 8 hours later Mr Nicholas was still there practising the same putt.

'Jack!' he said incredulously, 'What are you doing, you've been practising that putt for 8 hours, you must be mad.'
Mr Nicholas looked up and said,
'Oh, I just want to see how my putting stands up when I get really tired'.

I've read about jugglers who have juggled and drilled a move until their hands have bled, Michael Jackson practises a new step until he passes out and whilst

I'm not recommending that you go to those extremes I do recommend that you take the technique through all of the pain and cut off points that the majority stop at, if you want to be better than other people, or fitter than other people or more knowledgeable than other people or more successful than other people then you have to train harder than other people, go out and train when other people think it is unreasonable to train and drill techniques to extremes that others cannot match.

When I was training for my ABA coaching certificate I would do ten thousand jabs, move around a circle, clockwise and anti clockwise one thousand times to get the footwork right.

At one of the gradings that I took at my club one of the younger students, Garry, performed badly at his boxing sparring basically because boxing frightened the pants off him, he'd got so bad that he was going to quit training because of his fear. After his grading, he just about managed a pass, I gave him some homework to be done before I would allow him to grade again in 12 weeks time, he had to complete 420 rounds of boxing sparring, at the club or at home, this worked out at about 5 rounds a day for three months. He reluctantly agreed (he had no choice - I wouldn't let him grade otherwise).

In the preceding three months I witnessed a metamorphosis, the shy lad that was frightened of contact had become not only a very competent boxer he had also realised bags full of confidence and the knowledge that his fears could be met and defeated. He became one of the most feared, respected and polite members of my club, at only 15 years of age - it was the drilling that did it.

I also remember as a young Karataka being constantly taken off my feet by my friend Paul's front lunge kick. I had no answer to it and he, or anyone else that used that technique against me, picked me off at will. To overcome the problem I spent one hole day with another friend, my instructor at the time Alan, firing the same kick at me again and again - a whole day. At the start of the day I got kicked all over the shop, by the end of the day my friend couldn't catch me a single time. Within one day (one very long day) I had turned a weakness into a strength by isolating and drilling. When I went back to the club the next session Paul could no longer catch me with his famous lunge front kick, nor could anyone else. So drill drill and drill again.

Here are a few suggestions, these are some of the drills that I use, though not all of them. Make your own drills up, nothing is cast in stone, you can drill anything from five minutes to five hours, many sessions I will go in to my club and have my people do nothing but one technique on the pads, maybe a right cross or a left hook or whatever, for the whole session. One thing is for sure - the more time you spend on a technique the better it will become and the quicker you will acquire the 'feel' (the 'feel' is impossible to articulate, it is an intangible something that comes when you work a technique to distraction). You cannot give someone the 'feel', they can only acquire it themselves by putting in hundreds of hours flight time. The drills are performed with a compliant partner.

Note:
Details of the technicalities of the following escapes can be found in the latter chapters.

Drills from scarf hold; Legs up and sit up

Throw your legs up in to the air and use the momentum to sit up, as you sit up sit through into scarf hold, your opponent does exactly the same and ends up in scarf hold. Keep drilling back and forward - 50 reps each side.

Hug and bridge

As you bridge the opponent over sit through into scarf hold and let the opponent do the same back, keep it smooth, back and forward, and repeat for 50 reps each side.

Poke and hook

Poke and hook the opponent's head and sit up and through into scarf hold and let the opponent do the same back the other way. 50 reps each side.

Drills from the Mount position:

Arm & leg tie and bridge

When you bridge the opponent over you'll end up in his scissor guard, climb through into the mount, the partner then repeats the same tie off and bridge, climb through back to mount - then you start again. Try to keep it smooth and continuous - 50 reps each side.

Bridge behind & arm grab

After you have bridged the opponent off and rolled him over you will end up in the scissor guard, climb through and into the mount and let your partner do the same. Again keep it smooth and continuous for 50 reps each side.

Drills from the side 4 1/4 Hold down:

Hug and bridge

After you have hugged and bridged your partner off roll straight into the side 4 1/4 yourself and let him hug and bridge you in the same fashion, he too will turn straight into side 4 1/4 and repeat the exercise. The smoother the better and for 50 reps each side.

Sit up and bridge

Same again, after you have bridged the opponent go straight into side 4 1/4 and let the opponent repeat the exercise, he too will go straight to side 4 1/4 then you repeat the exercise again for 50 reps each side.

Drills from Upper 4 1/4 Hold down:

Bench press and bridge

When you bench and bridge your opponent you will end up in the upper 4 1/4 from where the opponent can bench and bridge you and then you he, etc. for 50 reps each side - keep it smooth and continuous.

Grab groin and bridge

Again, when you bridge your opponent you will end up in the upper 4 1/4 from where the opponent can bridge you and then you he, etc. for 50 reps each side - keep it smooth and continuous. You don't have to actually grab the groin in this exercise, just simulate - there are only so many times that you can grab a man by the testicles before the exercise goes completely out of context.

The important thing with these drills is that, even if they don't start that way, they should get progressively smoother - this is when you know that you are getting the exercise off - remember that you are doing this with a compliant partner and that at some point the compliancy must go and you need to practice with a partner who is trying to stop you from escaping - all-out ground fighting is the best time to do this but, you can also isolate pins and practice trying to escape with the partner trying to stop you. This will be good practice for you in securing escapes and also for your partner in holding pins.

Note:
There is no substitute for actual all-out fighting on the ground, no matter how much time you spend drilling a technique against compliancy it will not

help you against un-compliancy so be sure to include as much all-out stuff as you can.

Conclusion

So, there it is, Volume Two. It is by no means an exhaustive text, many of the best escapes you will learn will be bastardised forms of the latter escapes and, as long as they work under pressure the more the better.

The empirical ones, that is the ones that you find yourself in your own sparring, will be the best ones, use these herein then as a template or the cloth by which you cut your own suit of techniques. What you don't want to be is a clone, my physique-strength-personality etc may be very different from yours so you may have to vary or adjust the technique slightly to suit - just because it works for me this way does not mean that it will work for you so use a little artistic licence, there are no barriers here, I am not restricting you to a certain style or a certain technique, as far as I'm concerned 'if it works-use it'. Thanks for reading, I hope that it has been of use to you.

Real Self Defence

Geoff Thompson

This complete illustrated manual includes a full range of techniques together with advice on awareness and avoidance of threat, fear control, weapons, law, and adrenalin switches. Also included are enlightening interviews with convicted muggers and their victims.

235 x 156 mm 176 pp ISBN 1 873475 16 0
£12.99 Paperback

Real Grappling

Geoff Thompson

Grappling is probably the oldest genre of combat known to man. This extensively illustrated manual takes you step by step through all the moves and techniques needed to become competent in the grappling arts.

235 x 156 mm 176 pp ISBN 1 873475 21 7
£12.99 Paperback

Real Punching

Geoff Thompson

Learn to pack a powerful punch with this illustrated manual that includes all the necessary moves and techniques to become competent in the punching arts.

235 x 156 mm 176 pp ISBN 1 873475 26 8
£12.99 Paperback

The Pavement Arena

Adapting Combat Martial Arts to the Street

Geoff Thompson

This illustrated manual takes the martial artist step by step through everything necessary to convert their skills for use in the 'street'.

235 x 156 mm 128 pp ISBN 1 873475 11 X
£9.95 Paperback

Real Kicking

Geoff Thompson

The realities of kicking in the street scenario are unveiled once and for all in this concise, professional, and down-to-earth book. All the moves and techniques needed to become competent in the kicking arts are included in this illustrated manual.

235 x 156 mm 176 pp ISBN 1 873475 31 4
£12.99 Paperback

Real Head, Knees and Elbows

Geoff Thompson

The final book in the **REAL** series, this volume includes devastating head, knee and elbow techniques from every range.

235 x 156 mm 176 pp ISBN 1 873475 77 2
£12.99 Paperback **September 1996**

Animal Day

Pressure Testing the Martial Arts

Geoff Thompson

Animal Day explores the myths about what does and does not work on violent streets. The reader is educated in all aspects of pressure testing the martial arts to ensure that character and technique are not lacking when a situation becomes 'live'. As seen on Channel 4's **Passengers**, **Loaded** Magazine, **Maxim** Magazine, **MAI** Magazine etc

245 x 190 mm 102 pp ISBN 1 873475 18 7
£9.99 Paperback

Weight Training for the Martial Artist

Geoff Thompson

This illustrated book shows the routines that helped Geoff become one of the world's leading martial artists. Whatever your art there is a routine in this book that will give you the muscular armour to place you a cut above the rest.

245 x 190 mm 104 pp ISBN 1 873475 13 6
£9.99 Paperback

On The Door

Further Bouncer Adventures

Geoff Thompson

The violence is graphic, the stories insightful and the laughs are plentiful as Geoff recalls four years on the door at a notorious establishment where violence was the norm.

216 x 135 mm 192 pp
ISBN 1 873475 72 1
£12.99 Hardback **September 1996**

Bouncer

Geoff Thompson

Sequel to **Watch My Back**, with more witty and violent bouncer stories. Geoff recounts his experiences with compelling wit and irony.

"Everyone in the country should read Geoff's work: it's both powerful and disturbing."
BBC Radio 4

216 x 135 mm 208 pp
ISBN 1 873475 04 7
£14.99 Hardback

Watch My Back
A Bouncer's Story

Geoff Thompson

The original cult classic. A story of mental and physical triumph over adversity at the front line of some of the world's roughest clubs.
    "Anyone wishing to overcome their fears of violence and life must read this book."
Muscle Magazine
    As seen on BBC1, ITV, Channel 4, SKY, Radio 1 & Radio 4.

216 x 135 mm 176 pp
ISBN 1 873475 03 9
£12.99 Hardback

**KARATE BOXING KICK BOXING GRAPPLING
COMPETITION TRAINING IT'S ALL AT**

COMBAT GYM

COVENTRY

Open Monday to Friday 9am -10 pm
Saturday & Sunday 10am - 3pm

For Information on classes
Tel: 01203 676287

PRIVATE TUITION AVAILABLE

ask about our
OPEN COMPETITION CLASS
Proprietors: Ian McCranor & Jim Burns

COMBAT GYM
WINSFORD AVENUE
ALLESLEY PARK COVENTRY